GW00789898

THE INVENTION
OF MORNING

Other books by the author

Poetry
Accidents (1974)
Short Stories (1978)
Three (1978)
Maida Vale Elegies (1983)
Journal (1987)

Fiction
Fugitive Aromas (1979)
Obsequies (1979)
Blown Footage (1980)
Delayed Frames (1985)
Dissolving Views (1986)
26½ Things (1996)

Graphics
The Glacier in the Cupboard (1995)

THE INVENTION
OF MORNING

and other poems

IAN ROBINSON

1997

Published by Redbeck Press,
24 Aireville Road,
Frizinghall,
Bradford BD9 4HH.

Design and print by Tony Ward
Arc and Throstle Press
24 Nanholme Mill, Shaw Wood Road,
Todmorden, Lancashire OL14 6DA

The Invention of Morning
ISBN 0 946980 40 3

Redbeck Press acknowledges financial assistance from Yorkshire
& Humberside Arts.

Acknowledgements

Many of these poems first appeared in the following magazines,
most still active, some now dead: ALLY (San Francisco), ANGEL
EXHAUST, AT LAST, BLADE, BLUE CAGE, BOGG, GIANTS
PLAY WELL IN THE DRIZZLE (New York), GREEN LINES,
HEADLOCK, IOTA, JOE SOAP'S CANOE,MALENKA, NEW
HOPE INTERNATIONAL, NINETIES POETRY, OSIRIS
(Massachusetts), OUTPOSTS, PAGES (1st series), POESIE
EUROPE (Frankfurt-am-Main), POETRY NOW, THE POET'S
VOICE (2nd series, Salzburg), RAMRAID EXTRAORDINAIRE,
RESPONSES, THE RHEATER, RUSTIC RUB, SCRATCH,
SEPIA, SMOKE, TEARS IN THE FENCE, TERRIBLE WORK, 3
x 4, THE WIDE SKIRT and THE WOLLY OF SWOT; as well as
in the collections MOTLEY FOR MOTTRAM (Writers Forum &
Amra Imprint, 1994), PORTFOLIO POETS, PUTNEY (Portfolio
Press, 1978), THE SMALLEST POETRY FESTIVAL IN THE
WORLD (Ship of Fools, 1994) and THURSDAY EVENING
ANTHOLOGY (Salamander Imprint, 1977).

CONTENTS

Part Four

Part Five

"The world is everything that is the case."
(Ludwig Wittgenstein)

"It is scarcely to be doubted that on many occasions we make the music that we imagine ourselves to hear."
(Dr Samuel Johnson)

PART ONE

AFTERNOON ON THE JODENBREESTRAAT : 1648

Light changes
>>each second jumps away like an easy fish
>>>caught but escaping always
a silence expanding in the empty room
>>as if borne by the thick ochre light
>>>through the upper half of the tall window
above the Breestraat
>>and a rattle of plates drifting up
>>>from two floors below the 'groote Schilderkammer'
the large studio where the canvasses wait
>>stacked against the high moulded fireplace –

>>>This rectangle of paper finished at last
(though it's never finished)
>>the model gone though the drawing remains
>>>on top of the pile of others
on the makeshift table –
>>two trestles two broad planks
>>>covered by a ragged canvas –
that moment fixed in time forever
>>but in a different light
>>>diffused by the small convex panes of glass
held together by their filigree of lead –
>>pen and ink and bistre wash
>>>a touch of white bodycolour
for the highlights of the flesh
>>205 by 190 millimeters
>>>and Hendrijke's downstairs now
with her cups and pans
>>but here she's still sitting
>>>naked to the waist
on the stool at the table below the window
>>cloth bunched around her hips
>>>the tattered grey upper curtain pinned back
to give a strong top light –

almost a study in 'contre jour' –
    with the easel in shadow
on the other side of the room
    and (as he should be, of course)
        the artist invisible behind it

And always it's the fall of light
    on the body that's important
        the weight of the flesh
the slip of light over a rounded thigh
    across a sloping shoulder
        and there it is – one more nude
to join the pile of others on the table
    a whole year of nudes
        and only one painting
Hendrijke as Bathsheba
    with King David's letter
        a real figure at last
without mystery
    not an invention
        and that little oil on wood
of the woman bathing
    lifting her slip up high
        too high Jan Six says
but he's a prude and public man
    who never sees the freer brushstrokes
        that indicate a new beginning
the articulation of form out of nothing
    the quick sweep of the palette knife
        a strip of brown
a hint of blue on the thick cream
    to show the bunched bottom of the cloth
        hitched up above the contrast
with that darkness where the thighs
    begin to close together
        that secrecy that's always there
lit now not then
    by this gelid yellowing light

like the wide afternoon sky
at Jaaphannes on the Diemerdyke
at Six's country place
looking out across the River Y
to Spaandam on the far shore
a place of silence rest
the light always changing
in flux under that wide open sky –

Reworking the forms
emptying their secrets out on to the paper
so many visions to recapture
the woman leaning out of the studio window
Hendrijke again and again
the fire billowing round the old Town Hall
the memory of that squat windmill
on the quai at Leyden
each picture resolving
turning into another version of itself
the flesh altering its colour
and its volume
not flesh at all
but substance to be mastered

And now the Breestraat silent for once
in the pale light of a late autumn afternoon
before the sun sets
before the world drifts into another dimension
and there on the paper
Hendrijke caught for a second
in that clear top light
on the folds of flesh at the belly
on the angle of the neck
on the sweep of hair at the shoulder
all these matter
all these things
can be made to last for a moment

and in a moment that is always part of another
       always a retreat from the real
to summon up the real again
       like a fish
              held for an instant in the net
and then jumping away into freedom
       into silence
              into another world
out of chaos into the light
       from the known back into the unknown

Part Two

CHANGES

I don't need anything, he said, this silence
is just right. The dead mouse lay in its box
on the table top. He watched a fly settle on the wall.
Everything had been described quite clearly,
there was little left to know. He opened the window,
peered at the night, and remembered
the bent stick he had thrown over the clifftop
that afternoon. Colours, he noticed, were fewer now,
even a branch shaking in the wind opened
a door and instead of recognition
there was only the sound of the sea.
Through the empty window, a crowded sky,
the odour of damp grass and voices coming nearer.

YESTERDAY

Darkness. No moon or stars at all.
Only the hiss of silence, a sense of space
hovering above. He lay in bed
and counted cracks in the ceiling.
Beside him, the single lamp; in his head
the babble of an immense confusion
that would not let his thoughts begin.
Daring to move, he put out a hand
towards the lampshade, but then drew back.
The lamp was warm, like forgiveness,
like a loving smile, but in everything
he touched there was the taste of yesterday.

CONFUSION

The light thickens, turns yellow.
We have plenty of time.   The teapot
waits on the table, the cutlery
and plates are carefully arranged.
It is a miracle that we are here at all.
In the street, lights stutter on.
In our hair, a scent of autumn,
dead leaves, the quiver of farewells.
How simple everything would have been
if we had never opened the door.

DISCOVERIES

The moon rose like a skeleton's head.
She curled up on the bed so that he did not know
if she were sleeping or sulking.

He watched an ant creep across the table top.
It paused at a crust, then zigzagged back and forth.

Later she told him stories
that aroused both jealousy and fear.

The night was full of interruptions.
He imagined he could read her thoughts
through the skin of her forehead,
through her closed eyelids.

At six am he went outside.
Surrounded by the light, the sky,
the yellow green water of the lake,
he discovered that he felt less guilty.
He tried to whistle but no sound came.

GARDEN AT EVENING

He forgot about the dust on the floor
and crumbs on the kitchen table,
the shrinking light behind the windows.

It started with the garden,
ashes from the dead bonfire,
cracked fencing and the clumps
of ragwort, flowering quince, camellias
waiting for something to happen.

Then darkness arrived
as smooth as falling water.

Sometimes, for minutes at a time,
the shred of a sensation, words
half-forming into thoughts, drifted
like blown sand across his mind,
a noise no different from silence,
obliterating time and presence.

CLAIMS

When he closed the door of his room he realised suddenly
that this space was exactly what he wanted, shut off
from the night outside, free from the claims of other people.
He looked at his face in the mirror to discover who he was.
Yes, that was all right.   But then, this scrap of paper
by the door, who left this message?

POSITIONS

"Look at that butterfly," she said.
They walked uphill, but he kept looking back
down the path, remembering the small
brown toad he'd nearly trodden on,
the way cloud shadows raced across
the white cubes of houses in the valley.
"What do you really want?" she asked.
The path was dusty, full of sharp stones,
a slope of fir trees reared above them
on the left. No words came to his mind.

At last they reached the lake. Above them,
trees ended and bald grey rocks
jutted upwards to the sky. From the centre
of the dark water a brown rock stood
straight up, something left over
from a time before this time. It has outlasted
all the years, he thought, snow, rain and frost,
the heat, it is afraid of nothing,
and unlike us it does not need redemption.
But her face offered him no clues.

All he needed now was just one word,
a single sentence maybe, nothing more.
He watched her hand pick up a pale brown stone;
and, at that moment, a screech came high and clear
out of the rocks above them and echoed round the water.

SILENCE

Silence
in a living room
a naked girl
cuts strips
from a blanket
a man
with a luminous
eyepatch
slowly
licks his fingertips
as the outline
of a hand
diffidently
draws circles
on the window.

TUESDAY : 12.15PM

The ferns in the glass outhouse
wave moodily at the sun;
the wind is falling off the roof.
In here, the starved spider
in the jam jar is preserved
like an ancient monument
and the air folds itself in half
between the crack in the mirror.
Each time I forget, I dream
of waves lapping the shore.
The guppies in the tank
wish they were pictures
in a book of symbols.
And the lines on my palm
trace out journeys never taken.

BLUES

Cold Sunday morning.
I look at the telephone.

There's a woodlouse
on the third floor ceiling.
I have been washing my hands
quite a lot lately.

The telephone rings, a wrong number.
At first, the woman at the other end
wouldn't believe me.

Well, of course.
"It's just a big shit sandwich,"
Crispin used to say.

But think of all the good things.
List them in a little book.
Then throw the book on the fire.

"He spent the whole of his life
coming out of the kitchen."

FIVE SMALL POEMS

1.
Gusts of leaves on pavements,
a sound like someone sweeping up paper.
Someone's playing a piano, too,
I can't keep quiet about that.

Streets transfixed in
the yellow stare of lights.

I am leaking like a
frayed rubber garden hose.

This minute will be called ....

2.
Is rhetoric what we need?
When I see a blackbird
on the lawn
I think of glaciers
but really
I am concerned
about my left shoe.
Then it starts
to rain again.

3.
"A view
of the fortifications."

It was not
what we wanted
but the postcard
was all we had.

Suddenly there were trees
lining the hilltop.
They had to do.
Is that a quarry?

Tomorrow we shall
see the waves.

4.
Here is the knife.
Here is the fork.
This, on the other hand,
is a plate.
If I try hard enough
I can exorcise them all
with a word.
A look is no use.

Where is the meal?

5.
A walk round the grounds.

A chicken wanders across the lawn.
Look, it's over there under the trees.
A tug hoots on the river.
Three ravens shout at each other
over the Bishops' ex-palace.

Have we gone too far?

PAST AND PRESENT

Perhaps it is an act of courage
simply to be here at all.

Curtains are drawn over lighted windows
beyond which couples are sitting down at tables.
Light glints on carefully placed wine glasses.
Framed prints of racehorses hang on the walls.

I swallow the second it takes
to look into the mirror.
And now, in the photograph,
we stand beneath slim birch trunks
watching something miles away to the left:
memories of flags and silence.

It is strange to think that the window,
through which we can watch the street lights
poised like giant planets,
is only only a kind of mirror too.

There are still dreams of permanence
in dusty corners of the empty hall.

SPACE

Finally everything was set.   The sun was in the sky,
the clouds in the window.   The window in the glass bowl.
The ivy on the floor.   The brassière over the back of the sofa.
The sentences in his head.   But somewhere
a bird swooped from a tree, a hand moved a glass.
In the mirror nothing was quite perfect.

SMALL SEPTEMBER POEM

(for Philip Crick on his 70th birthday)

That afternoon a flock of goldfinches dropped down
into the garden and spent five minutes pillaging
the purple Cosmos flowers before they flew away.
From the couch where he lay indoors, a blanket to his chin,
he could not see them but could easily describe
their busy progress in his mind.   On the walls,
pictures – an Ostend beach scene, a still life,
a lightly tinted photograph of the Thames in 1906 –
watched him and waited for his attention.
Eyes closed, he searched his mind for a word
that would explain the present moment,
and reveal the secret processes of our lives.
He knew that every second something altered in the world,
that the goldfinches had left the garden for another year,
that the clouds roared noiselessly above the house;
that in all this confusion a moment would declare itself,
an explanation dawn behind his patient eyes,
to fill the room with the mystery of music
and open up the spaces between the invisible stars,
making them and us conscious of each other;
and, since life is more than being here and bearing witness,
rewarding them with an existence puzzling as time
and short as the garden where the Cosmos flowers
now waited to be reborn virginally next year.

Day with 'Flu

All day a sensation of damp, wet walls
a grey film of water over the window, the trees
beyond moving like ghosts.   When the sun came out
birds cocked their heads, swooped down from rooftops
and flew away.   Puddles reflected rippling sky.
At evening, a tentative wind gusted across the streets
and penetrated the room where he lay
fluttering the corner of the poster on the wall
gently twitching the papers covering the bed
and mesmerized him by the distance it had come.

Visit

Nobody was about downstairs.
'Sit there,' she ordered, 'I'll bring you something hot.'
The room was filled with trophies : a jewel box
made of sandalwood, embroidered cushions,
an armadillo skin basket and several boxes
of Egyptian mummy beads.   And on the mantlepiece,
photographs of 1930s film stars in aluminium frames.
He could not move for objects.
He thought of his uncle's sudden stroke
and Poe's 'Tales of Mystery and Imagination.'
Somewhere a dog barked and glasses tinkled.
And, oppressed by a feeling of security and despair,
he waited for her steady, returning hand
clutching hot chocolate.   He could already sniff the steam.

ANATOMY OF THE GALLOP

Undeniably, the acrobats have ceased to entertain
even though we continually expect fresh revelations.
I suppose I ought now to ask you for a smile
but you are too preoccupied with this ritual.
And the nights are so soundless, so brilliant
with specks of starlight and so on, that no one dares
to venture out after the dark declares itself.
Objects on the mantlepiece in the dining room
are awaiting our inevitable return from other delights
so that the longueur inside our heads becomes unnerving.

Briskly, we imitate ideas about everything.
But there are so many disparate pieces to each minute
that we believe everything should be changed, estranged.
The procession starts again.   I pronounce the word 'love'
and put the whole edifice in motion one more time
but without any clear perception of where sense begins
and the various tyrannies of meaning make an end.
Nights of iron and seconds made of skin :
small stifled cries drift over the garden fence
across senseless and unimaginable distances.

FREIGHT ON BOARD

Suddenly nothing is incomparable anymore.
All yesterday we strayed among the ruins,
talking, taking snapshots, the grass was green and wet
and it was like midday all day long.
Nothing fitted, nobody told us who we were.
I have to admit that I said too many things
and that at night, sometimes, I even talk to myself.
There are no easy answers to such difficulties
and at times our desire for crude imitations defeats us.
I had no idea what was going to happen next
and watched the curtains sway in the elusive draught.
Later we stopped at the bridge and the cars rushed by
surprising our attention with their intrusiveness.
There comes a point when such nuances become unreliable.
In the morning I ate the sausages quite cold
as the voices of the others drifted faintly across the water.
When it was over, more words has been spilled
into the silence. Frantic, I reached for the map
but it told me nothing new. The cat had gone outside
and the empty streets floated on a sea of rain.

WAITING FOR THE GREAT OCCASION

From here you'll have a good view of the square.
You'll be able to see the carnival quite clearly.
Look at those cars – do you see that palace?
The bearded dwarf acrobats will come tumbling
down the street, followed by the elephants
festooned with multicoloured paper streamers,
the Snake Lady in a gilded carriage
and a floating tableau of the Battle of Omdurman –
all those shiny swirling Dervishes and long spears
catching the pale late-afternoon sunlight.
It will all be there, we'll see the whole show.
There are some days when the things of the spirit
are all that matter.   Haven't you noticed how the people
down there are all turning their heads to the left,
how the klaxons have suddenly gone silent?
"Anyone who doesn't love dogs doesn't love children,"
someone is saying.   Do you like Tchaikovsky?
I've got the thermos flask and the rubber cushion.
With luck, that rain poised over the distant
blue mountains will hold off a fraction longer.

THREE PM ELEGY

Do you remember yesterday?   It seems to us
to have had a distinctive resonance quite its own.
But now we're indissolubly here, positioned at just
this little hole in the map, and all we can do
is to make uncertain shapes out of the darkness.
Vicky combs her hair endlessly, John dreams of space ships
and, somewhere altogether else, the Duchess of Braganza,
out of her mind, trails down a damp cobbled lane
dragging a wrecked umbrella behind her.
Vistas of pleasure entice us : streets of idle women
in long dresses, men with shiny hair lounging at café tables.
"In those days, pomade was an essential part
of Argentine culture."   Yes, we remember that.
And, to the south, mountains and deserts, the hiss of firs
in vast wet forests, miles of snaking silver sand.
Poised above the end of the iron bedstead, in the white room,
the names are scratched in blue biro on the wallpaper,
whose pattern we can always claim to be another's choice :
Skelton, Hammerschmidt, Vernon, Maguire .....
blurred phone numbers, memories of the impossible.

READING BETWEEN THE LINES

"Now I've come to the wrong planet," he wrote recently
and these words propel us out into the world we think we know.
Our usual bland desire for crude, unfeeling substitutes
has an absorbing quality and it is by this process
that we are left with only a recollection of what once was.
Our lives offer us scattered distances: prolonged shadows
intrude into our certainties: are these shoes right? –
shall I wear a tie? Shall we speak of this, or even
of those occasions that refuse to show us anything new?
Of course, the skaters on the black pond have no such problems
because the snow has made everything quiet, and all the streets
are just the way they are because they grasp at our attention.
In this winter landscape, earthly things are getting tedious
and knowledge is only how we put these words together,
with our empiricisms untouched, our lives still enclosed
even though we keep a purchase on what makes us old.
The daylight, too, is thin and delicate, so tense with sounds
that twist our thoughts to interesting fragments. The shops
blaze with such possibilities that we have no room for anger
and our words speak in tune, though they are far apart.

A Moment in Time

By five in the afternoon everything is ready.
The short girl in green with wobbly breasts,
the erratic piano player in the drawing room above,
even my hand resting tentatively on the windowledge,
all these can claim their part in this enervating hubbub
so that the memory of those hectic winter nights
is not the only thing we have to sustain us.

The piano drops out of the window noiselessly,
and the green girl's breasts flop limply to her sides
as she lies back on the bed, waiting to be explained.
To the north, the expected migrations are taking place
and at evening here, the starlings rise in a flickering
cloud from the far-off elms by the side of the river:
oceans of eyes surround us and a trite sadness.

PART THREE

THE INVENTION OF MORNING

It's no use saying we have seen this before.
Look how the scene we are part of now
composes itself in a minute sequence of actions,
none of them preferable to any other.
And evidently too, as each moment succeeds the last
and we move further into this deviant process,
our differences become more noticeable after all.
Acts propose themselves before us, each one
suggesting further possibilities, but before
we can evaluate their promise something else
propels us further forward, our footsteps shifting
eagerly upwards on the springy turf coating
this field.   It is morning, intense and active.
Small balls of smoke drift up the hillside
and, further off, the girl stands in the shadow
underneath the pine tree, eager for surprises,
her hands clenching and unclenching on space;
everything unawares threatens her immobility:
our stares, the yellow cat dreaming
by an empty hole down the slope to the left,
even those far-off people in places we have left behind.
It is not that her stillness is disturbing but now
so many things seem possible in this largeness of air
that we have to shrug our shoulders in mild confusion.
Far below the rim of the hill, for instance,
small white cubes of houses peek temptingly
over the horizon behind her back, mere incidentals.
Even this reminder of the world is unhelpful,
especially in the uncomplicated light of morning.
Beneath the tree her outstretched hands turn slowly
palm-upwards as a lattice of shadow crosses her face.
Yes, of course, there is movement: the earth is turning
and the air drifts broodingly within this composition
so that we feel like going on even if she does not.
I look at you despairingly but you are trying
to find a language for these doomed appearances.
Among the birdsong and our words no one remembers
those non-events that altered us forever:

that moment of entry into the greenhouse,
the pattern of sunlight on a forgotten wall,
the dead porpoise on the beach, vivid with another
kind of life; and now we realise we have left
the sandwiches on the back seat of the car.
It is not that we do not belong here,
rather that the hands that touched us once
are part of us no longer and live in another dimension,
free of our introspection, and if we look about us now
there are other pointers to our lack of attachment:
on the beach footprints lead in a straight line
to the edge of the captious sea. To the left,
a flight of swifts zoom, without explanation,
down into a gully out of sight and there are wheeltracks
in the grass. Do you remember how it was?
How there were days when anything seemed possible,
how the curtains fell away to reveal
the faces of the quizzical-eyed clowns?
But this is not enough, it seems: we require
more evidence to anchor our certainties in this moment.
The field waits for us, and the tree, and the girl
beneath it, and we are here, leaping into the future.
It's no use wondering what she's doing there,
she has chosen her moment and our lives go on.
A ripple of wind runs from the pine tree,
beneath which her position has not changed,
to the edge of the cliff and falls over it to meet
the oncoming seagulls, destined for our naive eyes.
We turn away because there are no questions
and everything is made of glass this morning:
breathe too hard and the picture will disintegrate.
Soon, though, there will be shadows slipping
towards the beach and seconds when we catch our gaze
seeking itself in mirrors to find a cause.
Clouds will loom and darkness fall across the grass
and tomorrow none of this will be available.

PART FOUR

THE PAST

Those names etched
on dirty scraps of paper –
cries from a distance
left behind to spoil
and alter in the rain.
Objects outlast the stares
we give them, drifting through water,
asking the wrong questions.
Voices echo in the head,
their meaning peels away
like skin, like dream.
Opening doors, we enter
rooms full of women
where nothing casts a shadow
that's explicable, drowned
in the funeral of light.

TREASON

"Now I'm free of personal relationships
and all affection," was what she'd written
in the letter.   He turned the paper over
but there was nothing except a brown stain
on the other side.   The ink was faded,
the paper torn and creased around the edges.
Those words obsessed him: were they an admission
of defeat or a triumph of the will?
This dirty scrap of paper had somehow survived
the years to tease him with its ambiguity.
So much had vanished.   Beyond the window
the leaves on the apple tree in the garden
waved in the wind and a blackbird shot across
a patch of pearl grey sky.   These were the present
where he was, and nothing else: the table
at which he sat, the clock ticking on the shelf,
letters on the doormat, the cat at the window –
though he still felt it a treason to forget
what he could not now recapture: words,
love, lies, faces, the exact geography
of the past, real or imagined, to which he owed
much more allegiance than he could ever now admit.

ON DECK

At the stern of the pleasure steamer
As it crossed the bay, he took the photograph
From his pocket and examined it once more.

The face was, of course, familiar, captured
On the deck of another steamer somewhere else,
The sun gleaming, the gulls screaming overhead.
It was like her, yes. But somehow, now,
He thought of her as being taller,
Less round-featured, even more serious.
That open smiling mouth was not so full
As he remembered it in close-up on so many evenings
In those rented darkened rooms. She was surely
Better looking, now that he tried to bring her back.

To bring her back from all those years before.
The photograph was very faded, creased, bent
At the corners. Even the ship was different –
Today, no gulls, no sun streaking the water.

PAUSE

A blackbird's face in the apple tree: I rest mine
on the handle of the lawnmower. Nothing else
resembles the far corner at the bottom of the garden:
a sodden cardboard box, two broken flower pots
and a rusty shopping trolley among tall weeds –
that's where the hedgehog was buried one day.
A helicopter and a pigeon chase each other
over the chimneys. The bird and I look up,
trying not to see each other or the boy
next door spitting from his third floor window.
A leaf drops to the grass, the sun hides in a cloud:
after today there will be nothing like today.

AFTER THE FUNERAL

The night arrived. Nothing happened. There were clouds
shaped like clouds, no stars. At the teacher's funeral
in the afternoon, his sister and two friends stood
in the rain beside the priest. One held his umbrella
while he spoke in Latin. Wind whistled in the leaves
and flattened the grass. Trying not to look,
they waited for the brown urn to be placed in the shallow
hole filling with water behind the gravestone.
Later, they wiped mud from their shoes
and lights came on in shop windows, except for the one
that sold the dolls. They watched the dolls' eyes,
tiny points of light staring blankly at the wet street,
unwavering, and offering nothing in return
for the silence that had overcome their thoughts.

INTERMISSION

On the landing he stopped and listened.
Something rustled on the floor above.
The key was cold in his hand. He wished
he could hear voices but there were none,
not even in his head. Years went by.
There was no one in the front room down below,
only the photograph album open on the table.
For an hour he'd stared at views of places
he'd forgotten, people who were strangers now,
just lay figures from a different world.
No one dressed or gestured like that anymore.
In the hall the clock struck nine.
Was it night or day? He didn't know.
He could sense the house moving through space,
through a crack in time, while he waited,
poised between one life and another
as if he were a ghost of himself.

How It Is

Nothing lasts, nothing I can remember, he said -
the seasons fly past as quickly as birds,
colour merges with colour, the light with the dark,
today with other days, the sun with the moon.
Washing floats on the green line across the garden:
a blue shirt waving, a pair of socks and an old
tennis ball rotting in the long grass.   I don't hear
the chiming of the clocks anymore, or the fall
of a woodlouse from the wall.   One night, he said,
when I lit a match, I saw the shadow
of someone's hand on the ceiling, a ghost
from the past - everything else is forgotten
in the wind bowling empty junk food cartons
along the pavements into the future.

Being

Darkness
in a kitchen
a crawling
woman
licks
the black linoleum
a cat
with a raw
green
wound
is eating ants
while the shape
of a man
angrily
tears newspapers
in the corner

WAKING UP

big cheese
the Creation myth again

saw pylons
thrush between curtains
light, I think, blue
spores of dust

the book where I left it
in another dream
yesterday

open page
blank
like now

DIFFICULT MOMENT

Down below him the sea moved
like a heavy grey curtain.
Up here a few ferns waved
in the strong east wind.
He sat quite still and thought
how behind him the dirt road
lead away to other places.
He listened.   A thrush sang.
And even the sound of water
falling on to a pale stone
somewhere to his left
contained an hidden narration
he would rather not confront.

Not Quite Right

The table cloth was very white.
A fly buzzed on the window.
It woke him.   He looked around.
He recognised the rubber plant,
the German clock, the door knob.
but somehow the sky was too far off,
the puffy clouds reaching across
the hilltops meant less to him
than the decisive light piercing
the transparent glass on the table.
When it arrived the sunset surprised him.
There were no cars or laughter in the street.
He felt like a man leaning
against a wall who is too helpless
even to think of climbing up.
Soon there would be nothing here at all.

The Space

There are four flat perpendicular walls
they enclose a space to put things in
beyond the walls are air and light and clouds
the clouds are moving, charcoal, round
there is no blue between, beyond them
inside the space are chairs, a table and a bed
on the flat perpendicular walls are pictures
a mantlepiece with objects, lamps
inside the space are things put there to fill it up
teacups and cupboards, books and ashtrays
outside the walls the charcoal clouds are moving
while within two people walk about
open the holes in their faces to let sounds out
and touch each other in different ways
filling the space between now and the start of night.

DISAPPEARING

They walked round the far corner
and were gone: an empty street.
You could just see a few early stars
and something hooted on the river.
Roads ran off from here and vanished.
It was not an easy story to tell
and no one was about to hear it.
Time shrunk the remaining trees.
In the space between the lamps
lay complicated patches of silence.

HELPLESS

When the door closed, he vanished.
She remained sitting at the table,
the small lamp by her side.
Somewhere the woodwork creaked.
She tried to imagine trees, a bat
swinging from a beam, a sunset,
anything at all, but nothing
of that long and tedious summer.
If she moved the lamp now
something terrible might happen.
From corners of the room
silence stared dimly at her.
Outside cars passed by, and hours.

45

AT NIGHT

He lay on the bed and closed his eyes.
He did not think anymore about words.
Around him, silent, neglected objects:
half a cup of coffee on the floor by the bed,
a broken biro, a dirty comb, torn paper
and a watch that did not tick.
A cigarette burned itself up in the ashtray.
Now even the message he heard in the rain
dripping steadily from clogged gutters
on to the black shapes of fallen leaves
down there in the moonless garden
was not a simple one any longer.
Three a m: nothing was easy or silent.
Eventually, the pencil fell from his fingers.

THE WORD

Take the first word that comes
into your head, say it again and again
until it becomes something else.
If I write down this meaningless word now
nothing special will happen.
The tap might stop dripping, I suppose,
the ginger and white cat scratching
at the window might go away,
the light might change from grey to yellow.
Outside there is the blemish of a footstep
on the blank page of snow in the garden -
which helps a little.   It's 6.0am.
Yesterday I buried the dead bird
by the garden fence.   No one watched me.
In a minute I shall let the cat in.
It's at moments like this
that I would like to hear music.
We should ignore most things,
like the flailing of wings
or that imagined shout from across the street -
and here I am again faced by that word
and the rest of the sheet quite blank.

THE VISIONARY

A man sits in a room
fully dressed on the edge of the bed
a book open on his knee
in the rooms above and below him
people are sleeping
when a dog howls outside somewhere
the man looks up and closes the book
there is only one small light on in the room
cast into shadow on one side
his hands look like lumps of raw meat
a clock strikes 4.00 am
in the block of flats opposite
a woman crawls out of bed
and walks to the lavatory
it is morning and there is a wind
the dog is silent now
the man does not look at his book
he is thinking something
across the road the woman pulls the chain
the man does not hear her
he closes his eyes slowly
the woman climbs back into her bed
it is still warm
now it is five minutes past four
the man is still sitting on his bed
he does not look at the book again
he is cold
the minutes tick away inside his head

HUNGER

He walked into the room and saw
the three mirrors on the left-hand wall
reflecting nothing but the empty sky.

On the mantlepiece was a stuffed owl,
its dusty wingtips the colour of sulphur.
In the mirrors it was not raining yet.
A blue plastic raincoat hung behind the door
above a broken green umbrella.

The woman sat by the window.
Standing behind her, his hands
searched for reflections in her hair
since he could find none in the room.

AFTERWARDS

After the phone call, she put his photograph
face down in the drawer.   Then she cooked lunch.
That night, when the television went dead,
she stared at the glistening, empty screen
and could not remember his face.   The cat got up,
stretched and walked to the door.   There was wind outside.
'I must be getting old,' she thought
but made no move to go to bed

THE GAME

Without speaking they had placed
the three balls on the table
they had hung the round balloons
and cut-out paper faces on the walls
and by the bed they had stood
the life-size cardboard figures.

Three fishtanks glowing green
rested upon the chairs
and in one corner lay
a yellow cat licking its paw.

Light moved in the three glass balls
nothing now would seem like yesterday
the balloons would wrinkle, lose their air
the fish would gape and die
the paper faces yellow by the hour
the figures sag under their own weight.

And all the time beyond the window
someone in black was waiting
patiently for the game to end.

MEMORY

He folded the newspaper; saw the rain outside.
The tape recorder was playing Russian songs.
He stubbed out the cigarette; the glass
was covered with bright white dots of water.
It made a curtain beyond which
he could not recognise familiar trees across the road.
Whatever happened now was in another time.
He did not hear the music stop.
If anyone came in, his face would be
unknown, changed.

MORNING

She pulled back the curtains.   She saw the day.
Upstairs someone was cooking toast, feet on the ceiling.
"I feel normal," she whispered. Sunlight arrowed
through the window, a cat sat on a wall.
The light seemed to heal her worries.
"I'm still here,:" she said and saw her face in the mirror.
Acres of years stretched ahead,
this house could be anywhere at all.

PART FIVE

MOVING FAST BETWEEN THE LINES[1]

(three fragments after Zukofsky and In Memoriam)

I.

Truth's way all one where it begins[4]
in time through space the carbon laid down first
and only later feet on turf that first sea
dried up a desert of salt in one huge valley
buried now three hundred feet below
the muddy bed from then till now a new beginning
new after aeons awaiting perfection the slow
blink of a spatial eye 'not one death but many
not accumulation but change'[7] a progress
of ancestors plate movement endless seasons
to scale the now our moment in time
today three birches outlined against the shore
freighters lined up in the long straight
under wide grey clouds these spores remain
behind sweet wrappers our plastic and our madness
black logs on the grey sandy beach a life
returning to itself inside a problem stated
a picture of the end and on the outside[2]
only a sole thrush voicing its freedom
the sky grey above the freighters painted
on the horizon these are what is given
what is ourselves blind but not from darkness[7]
but moving within this time a peace
waiting for its end a shadow lifted
the last threatened note of speech.

II.

Inside this little world[2] nothing but breath
'Yes, and then?' he asked[5] but the image
not a description[1] is what's needed
song against speech light against dark
one thing put against another[1] because
looking backward everything not the aim
is worthless so much dross except as respite[5]
what can be said is said again faces recalled
a lens focusing[3] in time through space
the sound of music through the open window
'Cape Cod girls they have no combs, Heave
away, heave...'[5] a world in the space between
each moment of these moments orchids storm
temples gardens in growing dusk 'a vinyardist'[5]
he said nurture the words say what one can
too little solace here to find out all 'the Truth'
giving up too little of ourselves like graves
lashed at by time and seasons and outlasting
all beneath their mounds desiring mastery[6]
over things but finding none within ourselves
the things possess us wait for us 'I'd like to ...'
he said[5] the sentence dying out like all the others
words falling step by step into a darkness
the shadow of a shadow a moment passing
and re-passing waiting out the night.

III.

Thought is now the time of coral
a thickening of light over water
a picture not a selective description[1]
the land green and expectant open
the winged wild geese who know the pathway[6]
cold current south warmer north[6]
once nothing here but cells forming
and re-forming in elemental tissue
only a momentary epiphany
stones piled high upon stones
two hundred paces round the cairn
each one a warrior's lament
marking this particular turf
for whoever has eyes to see it
a heap of stones will last forever
not the flesh on the fragile bone
two sacks full dug from the soil
on this spot seven bodies in a single
compartment cist grave
two in a double compartment cist
one unprotected with a pillar stone
raised four feet high above it
the maker's 3,500 year old thumb print
fixed in the fired clay of the pot sherd
we have walked a long way through the darkness
a peopled earth moving and changing
moving and changing in each perishable season[6]
bones laid down in a time before this time
those ancestors without number
one commodity replacing another[6]
mist autumn green nights tides
and sunsets the pull of the moon
it could be the last day of life
past the dead and past the living
and at last this is where we stand
shaped by knowledge finite as breath

we go the way of birds animals weather
a child learns on the blank pages[6]
an old man remembers nothing
the palimpsest continually restructured
a single breath upon the vastness
growing out again into the world.[2]

Notes

1) "I think I may move faster between the words than most
   people. And I never want to describe. I want to present
   things quickly by scenario or story. The image is not a
   description. You put one thing against another and the
   poem is its own little world again." (L.Z to Edward
   Lucie-Smith)

2) "I wanted it clear that there is a world outside, and if
   you want to be a poet you exist in it, and make your own
   little world which eventually goes back into the greater
   one." (L.Z. to Edward Lucie-Smith)

3) "An Objective: (Optics) - The lens bringing the rays from
   an object to a focus. That which is aimed at. (Use extended
   to poetry) - Desire for what is objectively perfect,
   inextricably the direction of historic and contemporary
   particulars." (from 'An Objective' in *Prepositions*, Rapp
   and Carroll, London 1967)

4) from *A 22 & 23*, Trigram Press, London 1977.

5) from *Ferdinand*, Cape Editions, London 1968.

6) from *All – the Collected Short Poems 1923-1958*, Jonathan
   Cape, London 1966.

7) Charles Olson